N is for Nature:
An Environmental Alphabet Book

www.greensugarpress.com

N is for Nature:

AN ENVIRONMENTAL ALPHABET BOOK

By Tim Magner   Illustrations by Mike Nudelman

Published by Green Sugar Press, LLC
Please visit us at: www.greensugarpress.com

Illustrations by Mike Nudelman
Book design by JustYourType.biz
Cover design by Dallas Drotz

Printed by Service Communication & Solutions (www.swoc.com) on a mix of post consumer waste
recycled paper and Forest Stewardship Council certified paper

Publisher's Cataloging-in-Publication data

Magner, Tim.
N is for Nature: an environmental alphabet book /
by Tim Magner; illustrations by Mike Nudelman.
p. cm.

ISBN 978-0-9820417-4-1

Summary: Introduces the letters of the alphabet through the wonders of
nature and the environment.

1. Nature--Juvenile literature. 2. Natural history—Juvenile literature.
3. Ecology--Juvenile literature.
4. Alphabet. I. Nudelman, Mike. II. Title.

QH48 .M28 2009

508.21--dc22
Library of Congress Control Number: 2008908376

10 9 8 7 6 5 4 3 2

A is for the Amazon Rainforest

See the exotic plants. Listen to the animals chirp, squeak and roar.

Wet and wild is the Amazon rainforest in South America.

Feel the tall trees. Breathe in the warm air.

B is for Bees

Buzzing from blossom to blossom and proving all insects aren't out to bug us.

Bees and plants go hand in hand.

Bees buzz, while other insects might march or crawl.

C is for Centipede

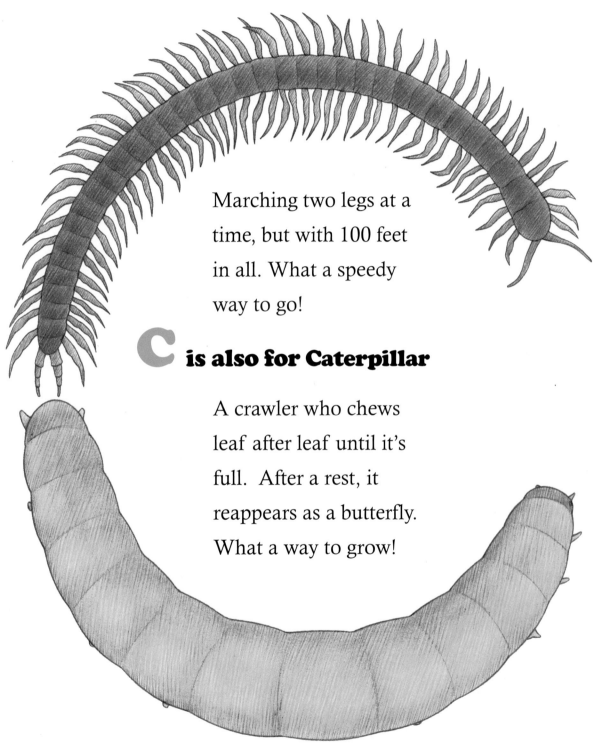

Marching two legs at a time, but with 100 feet in all. What a speedy way to go!

C is also for Caterpillar

A crawler who chews leaf after leaf until it's full. After a rest, it reappears as a butterfly. What a way to grow!

D is for Dinosaur

Long, long ago, the giant and mighty Dinosaur roamed and ruled the land. Today, only Dinosaur fossils remain.

E is for Earthworm

Without eyes, ears, or bones, Earthworms may look lowly.

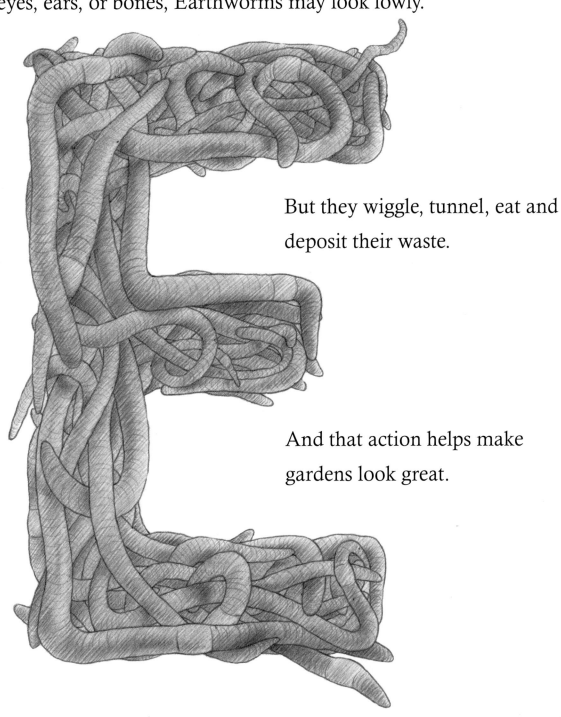

But they wiggle, tunnel, eat and deposit their waste.

And that action helps make gardens look great.

F is for Fish

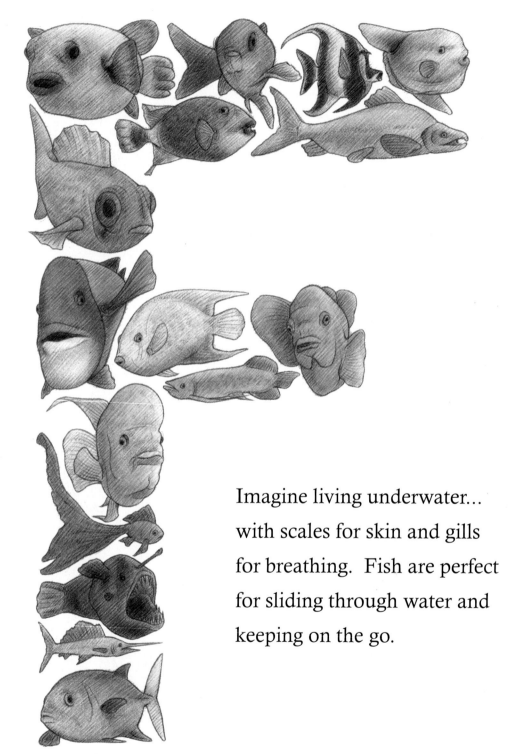

Imagine living underwater... with scales for skin and gills for breathing. Fish are perfect for sliding through water and keeping on the go.

G is for Great Apes

Gorillas, Orangutans and Chimpanzees– at home in the trees of forests. Here they chase, wrestle and tickle family members and friends.

H is for Habitat

Habitat describes the living place of a plant or animal.

All animals have homes where they have everything they need.

I is for Iceberg

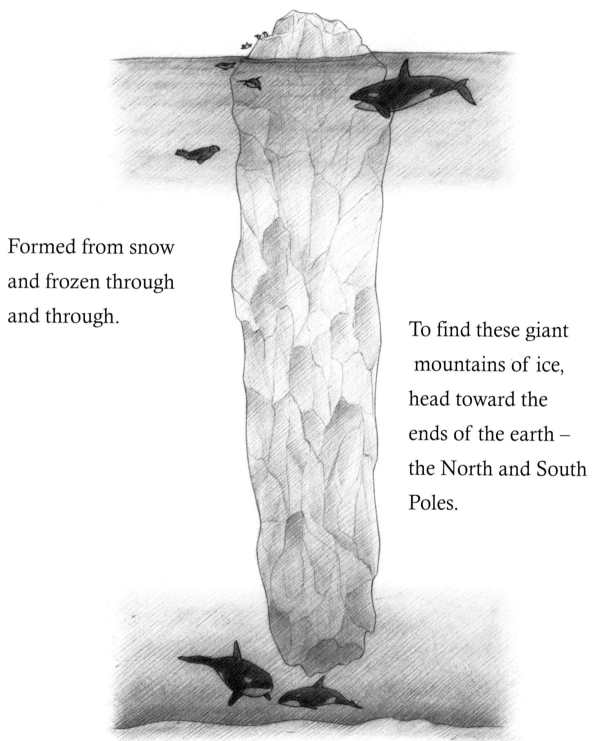

Formed from snow
and frozen through
and through.

To find these giant
mountains of ice,
head toward the
ends of the earth –
the North and South
Poles.

J is for Jaws

Chew, munch, nibble,
inhale, absorb, sip,
swallow, suck, or even
Jaws that rip.
Everything eats
differently. Eating
and drinking is
how we grow.

is for Kangaroo

Grazing on plants and leaves with
a Baby Joey in her pouch.

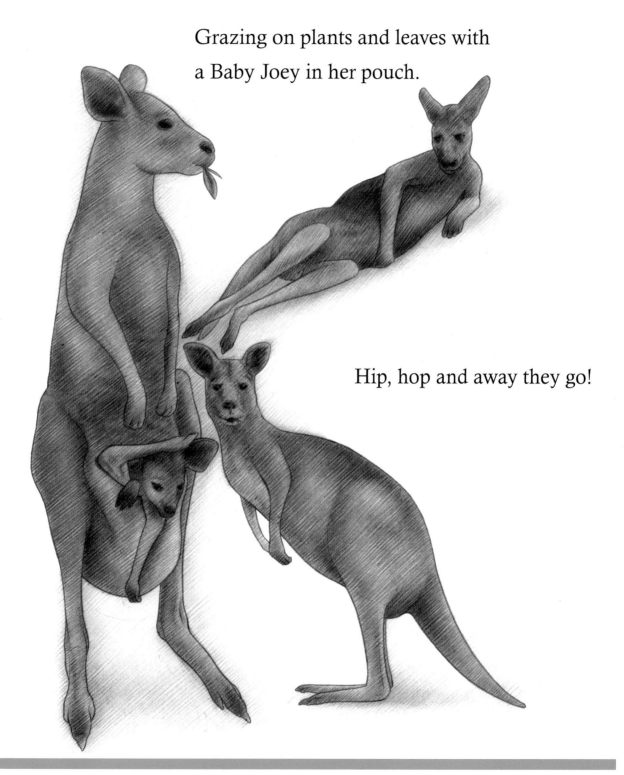

Hip, hop and away they go!

L is for Leaf

Living on sunlight,
making food, giving
shade, keeping cool.
The prettiest sight
may be a world full
of leaves.

M is for Migration

A long journey for animals to find better weather and more food and water.

All together now, they know where to go, once in the Spring and once in the Fall.

Here and there. There and here. There is no escaping it – what we eat, what we drink, what we see and what we breathe – it's all part of Nature. We are a part of it too.

O is for Ocean

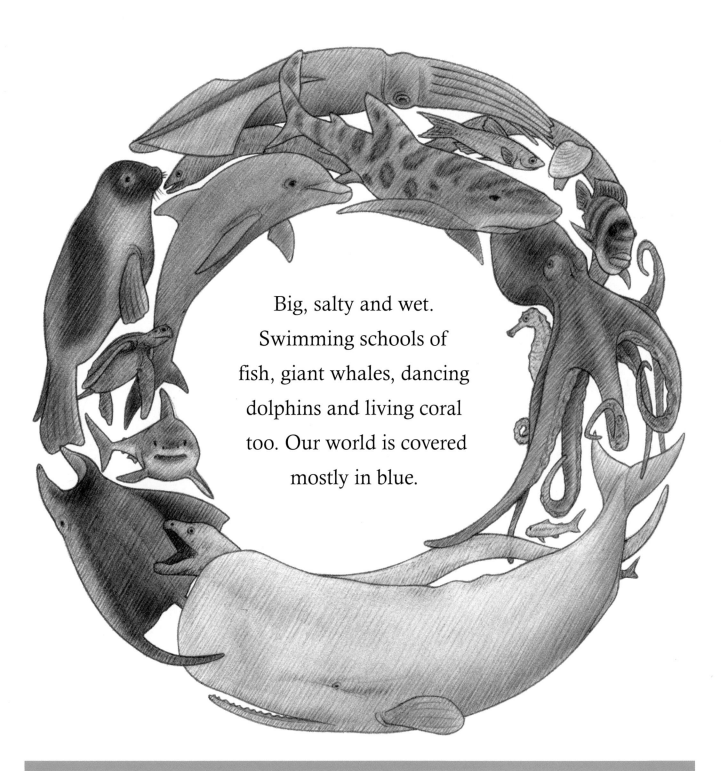

Big, salty and wet.
Swimming schools of
fish, giant whales, dancing
dolphins and living coral
too. Our world is covered
mostly in blue.

P is for Panda

No growling for this rare bear. Only quietly chewing on bamboo shoots and leaves in the misty mountain forests of Asia.

is for Questions

Examine, inspect, ask Questions and discover. Do it on your own, or do it with friends and family. It's the best way to learn about nature.

R is for Reptile

Dry, scaly skin covering bony skeletons. Turtles and tortoises.

Snakes and lizards. Crocodiles and alligators. The sun warms them all.

S is for Sun

Burning bright, full of heat and light.

The Sun is a star in the sky at the center of our solar system. The Sun makes the world go round.

T is for Trees

For the air you breathe, the water you drink and the forests you see, we say "Thank You" to our friends – the Trees.

Without them, there would be no you or me.

And they do all of this for free!

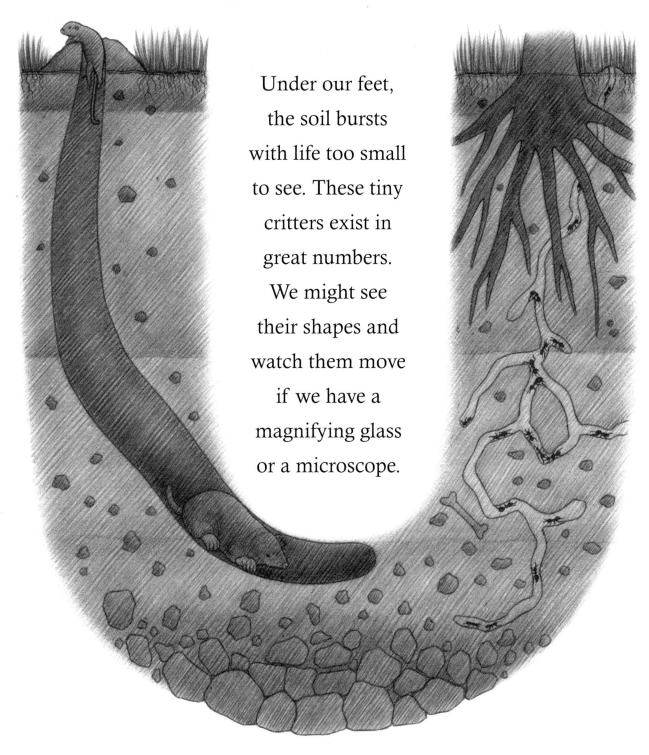

U is for Underground

Under our feet, the soil bursts with life too small to see. These tiny critters exist in great numbers. We might see their shapes and watch them move if we have a magnifying glass or a microscope.

is for Vision

During day or night, from near or far, or even underwater too.

Each animal in nature sees differently.

is for Wetland

Where rainwater settles so the ground becomes spongy. We also call a Wetland a marsh, a bog or a swamp.

Wildlife calls it paradise! But what does land with little water look like?

is for Xeriscape (pronounced 'zeriscape')

The word that describes the look of land with little rain. Xeriscapes often appear desert-like.

Y is for Yak

The world's largest cattle. Yaks graze on grasses high in the mountains of Asia.

When the weather freezes, they grow long, shaggy coats.

Z is for Zoo

A place to see animals from faraway lands. Brought to us, we shout and roar.

Want to find a Zoo for plants? Visit a Botanical Garden and learn what plants live near you.

Nature & Children

"If we want children to flourish, to become truly empowered, then let us allow them to love the Earth before we ask them to save it." —David Sobel

What are your first memories of nature? Making mud pies? Watching lightening during a thunderstorm? Swinging at a nearby park? Fostering a connection with nature is easier than you think. Encourage natural curiosity by taking children outside at an early age. Allow them to dig in the dirt, walk in the rain, listen to the birds, and watch the squirrels. Better yet, do it all with them. When they wonder, wonder with them. When they ask, ask back. Watch them, and help them discover a wonderful adventure—nature nearby.

- Nature is all around us. It's not necessary to take a camping trip to introduce children to nature. It's in the backyard, in the park down the street, even growing between the cracks in the sidewalk.

- We are part of nature too. Humans don't only affect the natural world, but we are also an important piece of the natural world. What we do greatly affects the nature around us.

- Nature is free. It doesn't cost anything to observe and explore the nature around us- the birds outside our windows, the worms in the garden, even the spiders in the corners.

- Experiencing nature early leaves a lasting impression. When children are outside, interacting with nature, they are building a base for science learning later in life.

- Nature encourages healthy childhood development. Studies have shown that exposure to natural elements calms anxiety, encourages creativity, boosts self-confidence, and aids in the development of leadership and other social skills.

THE PEGGY NOTEBAERT NATURE MUSEUM
The Museum of the Chicago Academy of Sciences

Through environmental and science education programs, The Chicago Academy of Sciences and its Peggy Notebaert Nature Museum inspire people to learn about and care for nature with the hope of encouraging Chicago residents and beyond to develop 'greener' living practices.

Shining light on the importance of nature. Visit us at *www.naturemuseum.org*